MW01491917

This journal belongs to:

____

Made in United States
North Haven, CT
14 September 2022

24135101R00061